W9-BRC-886

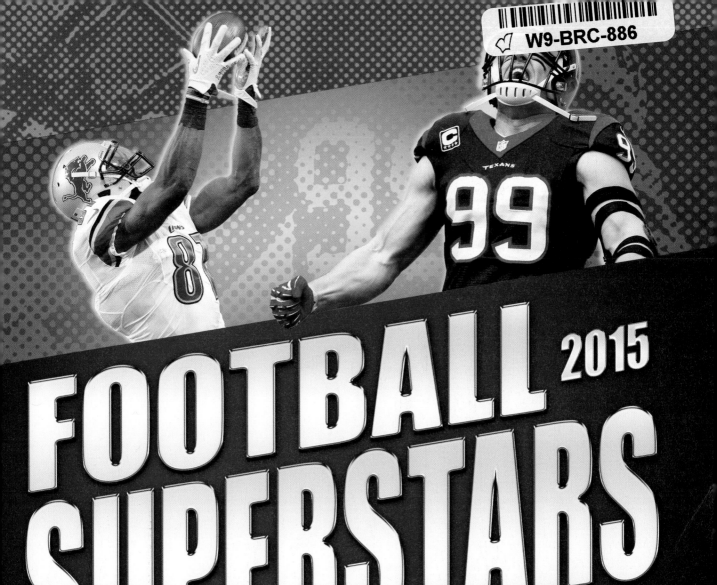

FOOTBALL SUPERSTARS 2015

SCHOLASTIC

Photo Editor: Cynthia Carris

Photos ©: cover top left: Otto Greule Jr./Stringer/Getty Images; cover top right: Scott Halleran/Getty Images; cover bottom left: Reed Hoffmann/AP Images; cover bottom right: Tom Dahlin/Getty Images; 1 top left: Tom Dahlin/Getty Images; 1 top right: Scott Halleran/Getty Images; 1 bottom left: Jim Mahoney/AP Images; 1 bottom right: Otto Greule Jr./Stringer/Getty Images; 4: Marc Serota/AP Images; 5: Marcio Jose Sanchez/AP Images; 6: Ronald C. Modra/Sports Imagery/Getty Images; 7: Phelan M. Ebenhack/AP Images; 8: Paul Spinelli/AP Images; 9: Boston Globe/Getty Images; 10: Kevin Terrell/AP Images; 11: Jeff Haynes/AP Images; 12: George Gojkovich/Getty Images; 13: Grant Halverson/Getty Images; 14: Tom DiPace/AP Images; 15: Chris Szagola/CSM/Landov; 16: Kevin Terrell/AP Images; 17: Kevin Terrell/AP Images; 18: Chris Humphreys-USA TODAY Sports/Landov; 19: Kevin Terrell/AP Images; 20: Todd Rosenberg/AP Images; 21: Tannen Maury/EPA/Landov; 22: Jason Pohuski/CSM/Landov; 23: Gene J. Puskar/AP Images; 24: Joe Robbins/Getty Images; 25: Michael Democker/The Times-Picayune/Landov; 26: Marcio Jose Sanchez/AP Images; 27: Jim Rogash/Getty Images; 28: Erik Williams/CSM/Landov; 29: Kevin Jairaj-USA TODAY Sports/Landov; 30 top: New York Daily News/Getty Images; 30 bottom: Grant Halverson/Getty Images; 31 top: Mike McCarn/AP Images; 31 bottom: Marcio Jose Sanchez/AP Images.

UNAUTHORIZED: This book is not sponsored by or affiliated with the National Football League, its teams, the players, or anyone involved with them.

Copyright © 2015 by K. C. Kelly

All rights reserved. Published by Scholastic Inc., Publishers since 1920. SCHOLASTIC and associated logos are trademarks and/or registered trademarks of Scholastic Inc.

The publisher does not have any control over and does not assume any responsibility for author or third-party websites or their content.

No part of this publication may be reproduced, stored in a retrieval system, or transmitted in any form or by any means, electronic, mechanical, photocopying, recording, or otherwise, without written permission of the publisher. For information regarding permission, write to Scholastic Inc., Attention: Permissions Department, 557 Broadway, New York, NY 10012.

This book is a work of fiction. Names, characters, places, and incidents are either the product of the author's imagination or are used fictitiously, and any resemblance to actual persons, living or dead, business establishments, events, or locales is entirely coincidental.

Library of Congress Cataloging-in-Publication Data available

ISBN 978-0-545-82642-6

10 9 8 7 6 5 4 3 2 1   15 16 17 18 19

Printed in the U.S.A.   40
First edition, September 2015

Book design by Cheung Tai

CONTENTS

*NOTE: ALL CAREER STATS TOTALS ARE THROUGH THE 2014 NFL SEASON

ANTONIO BROWN

Antonio Brown is one of the best receivers in the NFL. But he had to walk a long road to get there. He grew up in a rough neighborhood in Miami. Family troubles meant that he had to spend many months living with friends or neighbors. He even lived with his high school coach for a while. Brown played quarterback in high school, but not well or often enough to earn a shot in college. But he still dreamed of an NFL future. Antonio made it into Central Michigan University and walked on to the team. That means he was not recruited and had to try out. But his skills were so impressive that the coaches there gave him a scholarship soon after.

He made the squad and was named the freshman of the year in the conference. He played three years at Central Michigan. (NFL star defensive end J. J. Watt was a tight end on the freshman team with Brown!) Brown was also one of the best kick returners in the nation. But he came from a small school and is only 5' 10", not huge for a receiver. Still, the Steelers saw something in his speed and grit and chose him as the 195th pick in the sixth round of the 2010 draft.

Brown helped the Steelers reach the Super Bowl in his first season, mostly by returning punts and kickoffs. In his second year, he made the Pro Bowl as a returner. But he really blossomed in 2013, catching 110 passes and becoming "Big Ben" Roethlisberger's number-one target. This time, when Brown went to Hawaii, it was as one of the AFC's top receivers.

That hard road to the top, and all those sofas he slept on, finally paid off big-time in 2014. Brown led the NFL with 129 receptions and 1,698 yards, while catching a career-high 13 touchdowns. He had eight games with 100 or more yards receiving. In December, he was named one of the two receivers on the All-NFL All-Pro team.

Brown is not the biggest or the fastest receiver. But he might just be the toughest. Against every team's top defensive back, he always puts up big numbers, fighting for every yard and every catch. He fought to make it to the NFL . . . now he's fighting to stay on top. Don't bet against him . . .

Football FACT

Do you know your receiving letters? A wide receiver on the side that has a tight end is called the Z. A receiver on the side opposite the tight end is called the X. Another name for the X is split end.

Antonio Brown

Height:	5' 10"
Weight:	180 lbs.
College:	Central Michigan
Drafted:	2010

▶ STATS!

Receptions:	390
Touchdown Catches:	28
Receiving Yards:	5,259

ANTONIO BROWN

ARIAN FOSTER

As NFL teams prepared for the 2010 season, someone named Steve Slaton was the Houston Texans' star running back and Arian Foster was going to be watching from the sidelines. When the season ended, Foster was the NFL rushing yardage and touchdown champ and a Pro Bowl star. Slaton watched from the bench. Though no team drafted him after college, Foster had been waiting for this chance . . . and he made the most of it. Since then he's remained among the NFL's top runners.

It only seemed as if Foster burst out of nowhere to become an NFL star. He'd actually been aiming for that since he was a kid. He was born in New Mexico, where he told teachers he'd be an NFL player some day. He grew up in San Diego after moving there with his dad. In high school, Arian was a top runner and linebacker. As a senior, he racked up more than 2,500 yards running, receiving, and returning kicks. The University of Tennessee offered him a scholarship. Though he was clearly talented, the Volunteers didn't use him as much as they could. Their coach used several running backs, so Arian wasn't able to

put up huge numbers. As a result of that and some injuries, he was not drafted by any NFL team in 2009.

After spending most of his rookie year on the bench, Arian knew he had to make a move. During training camp, he worked harder than ever. When the starting lineup for the team's first game was announced, Arian was in there. Good move, Houston! Arian set a team record with 231 yards in that first game and never looked back. He led the NFL with 1,616 yards and 16 rushing touchdowns.

In the seasons since, he has topped 1,000 yards and made the Pro Bowl in every season except 2013, when he was injured for eight games. He led the league with 351 rushing attempts and 15 touchdowns in 2012. In 2014, he reached his 32nd game with 100 or more rushing yards. That is the most all-time by a player who was not drafted.

Arian is a great example of a player who found a way to be a star after being overlooked by every team in the NFL on Draft Day.

Football FACT

The NFL has been using its annual draft since 1936. The first player ever chosen in the draft was Jay Berwanger. The running back from University of Chicago was chosen by the Philadelphia Eagles. He decided to take a job in business instead of joining the NFL and never played in a game!

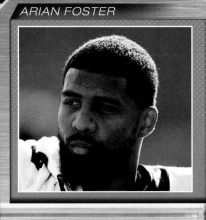

ARIAN FOSTER

Height:	6' 1"
Weight:	227 lbs.
College:	Tennessee
Drafted:	Not drafted

▶ STATS!

Rushing Yards:	6,309
Rushing TDs:	53
Receptions:	227
Receiving Yards:	2,041
Receiving TDs:	12

ARIAN FOSTER

ROB GRONKOWSKI

Almost all football players say they love to play. But few players seem to love it as much as the guy they call "Gronk"! The Patriots' All-Pro tight end always seems to be having a great time, on and off the field. Thanks to his pass-catching skills, Patriots fans have been having a great time ever since he joined the team!

Gronk grew up in New York State and Pennsylvania. He comes from a family of great athletes. Two of his brothers, Chris and Dan, are NFL tight ends as well, though not as accomplished as Gronk (but you could call them Gronks, too!). Another brother played college baseball, while the fifth Gronk brother is still in college . . . and yes, he plays football!

In high school, Gronk was a very good basketball player, but was also one of the best tight ends in the nation. He headed west for the University of Arizona, where he broke all the school records for tight ends. The Patriots thought he might be something special, and they chose him in the second round of the 2010 NFL draft.

Turns out they were right. Gronk scored 10 touchdowns as a rookie and then blew the doors off the NFL in 2011. At the age of 22, he set an all-time NFL record for tight ends with 17 touchdown catches. He also edged out New Orleans star Jimmy Graham for the single-season yards record, with 1,327. Few teams could figure out how to stop a guy who was this big and this fast and could catch this well.

In 2014, he led NFL tight ends with 12 touchdown catches among his 82 receptions. He was the only player who got 50 out of 50 votes for the NFL All-Pro Team. The big guy was back . . . and the Patriots were headed to the Super Bowl.

In that game, Gronkowski was huge. He had six catches for 68 yards, including a 22-yard scoring catch in the first half. His play helped the Patriots win Super Bowl XLIX, 28–24, over the Seahawks. Time to start another Gronk Party!

Football FACT

In the NFL, every position group has a set of uniform numbers it must choose from. All tight ends must wear numbers between 80 and 89, for example. Gronk is number 87. If those numbers are all taken, then a tight end can choose from 41 to 49.

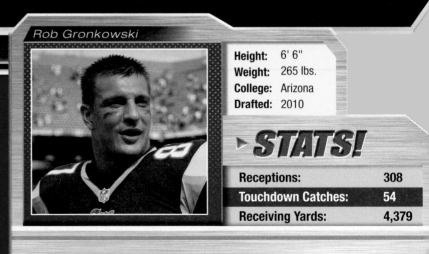

Rob Gronkowski

Height:	6' 6"
Weight:	265 lbs.
College:	Arizona
Drafted:	2010

▶ STATS!

Receptions:	308
Touchdown Catches:	54
Receiving Yards:	4,379

ROB GRONKOWSKI

CALVIN JOHNSON

Calvin Johnson became known as "Megatron" during his record-breaking seasons with the Detroit Lions, but he's been a big deal on the football field for a long time. A star in high school, he had many offers for college. Urged by his parents not to forget the books, he chose Georgia Tech, near his home outside Atlanta. By his junior year, he was the winner of the Biletnikoff Award as the best receiver in college and a first-round draft pick by Detroit.

He led the NFL with 12 touchdown catches in 2008, but the Lions were really struggling. Things turned around in 2009 with the arrival of quarterback Matt Stafford. The strong-armed young quarterback and the tall, lanky receiver made a perfect pair. By 2010, they were lighting up the scoreboard. In 2011, Johnson had a career-high 16 touchdown catches.

But as great as Johnson was, his 2012 season was one for the ages. The single-season record for most receiving yards had been set way back in 1995 by Hall of Famer Jerry Rice. By the middle of 2012, it didn't look like that record would be in trouble. But then Megatron picked up 207 receiving yards in a loss to the Vikings. He then reeled off six straight 100-yard-plus games. He capped the streak off with a season-high 225 yards against the Falcons. During that game, on a 26-yard pass from Stafford, he broke Rice's record. The game was stopped as he took the ball over to the sideline and gave it to his dad, Calvin Sr.

Johnson was not done setting records. In 2013, in a game against Dallas, he made 14 catches for 329 yards. That was a Lions record, but also the second-most ever in an NFL game. Best of all, the final 22 of those yards set up a game-winning touchdown dive by Stafford.

In 2014, Johnson was slowed by an ankle injury, but managed to keep his 1,000-yard streak alive. The Lions had one of their best seasons in years, winning eleven games (their most since 1991) and earning a wild card playoff spot. Though Detroit lost to Dallas, a healthy Johnson gives them a Megatronic leg up on returning for another shot in 2015.

Football FACT

Wide receivers are a huge part of the NFL today. That was not true in the early days. The NFL was twenty-two years old before Green Bay's Don Hutson became the first receiver to top 1,000 yards in a season (1,211 in 1942). Then only three other players did it before 1950!

Calvin Johnson

Height:	6' 5"
Weight:	239 lbs
College:	Georgia Tech
Drafted:	2007

STATS!

Receptions:	643
Touchdown Catches:	74
Receiving Yards:	10,405

CALVIN JOHNSON

LUKE KUECHLY

Luke Kuechly (pronounced KEEK-lee) grew up in Cincinnati and then played at Boston College. In three seasons there, he set a school record for tackles. His total was actually the third-most in NCAA history. As a junior, he won all the major defensive trophies, including the Butkus Award, Lombardi Award, and Bronko Nagurski Award. But he was also building a reputation for politeness and maturity that's not always seen in superstar athletes.

He was the ninth overall pick by the Panthers in 2012 and was immediately a starter. In a game against New Orleans in 2013, he recorded an amazing 24 tackles. That's tied for the most ever in a game since they started counting the stat in 1994. His 164 official tackles in the 2012 season led the NFL and he was named the Defensive Rookie of the Year.

But he was just getting started. In 2013, he was fourth in the NFL with 156 tackles. His ability to rove on both ends of the line to stop running backs, while also defending receivers, was awesome. When the season was over, he was no longer the top rookie on defense, he was the Defensive Player of the Year!

In 2014, he got even better, helping the Panthers to their second straight playoff berth. In the wild card game against Arizona, Kuechly was everywhere. He had a team-leading 10 tackles and picked off a pass. Late in the game, his deflection of a possible touchdown pass sealed the Carolina win. Though they lost the next week to Seattle, the Panthers were happy to see Kuechly named to his second straight All-Pro team.

Amid all this, Kuechly was taking online classes to complete his degree at Boston College. By summer, he was back signing endless autographs and patiently answering questions from reporters. He had a smile and a handshake for everyone . . . unless they were wearing the wrong jersey and carrying a football.

Football FACT

This linebacker's name is Luke, but every linebacker in the NFL is also called Will, Mike, or Sam. Those nicknames refer to "weak side" (the side away from the tight end), "middle," or "strong side" (on the same side as the tight end).

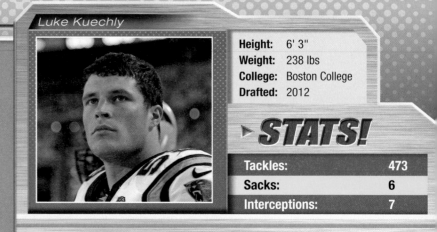

Luke Kuechly

Height:	6' 3"
Weight:	238 lbs
College:	Boston College
Drafted:	2012

▶ **STATS!**

Tackles:	473
Sacks:	6
Interceptions:	7

LUKE KUECHLY

13

ANDREW LUCK

Andrew spent part of his youth in Germany and England. But fortunately for the Indianapolis Colts, he didn't stay in Europe. Andrew's dad, Oliver, was a former NFL quarterback. When Andrew was young, Oliver helped run some teams that the NFL started in Europe to show people over there all about the game. Andrew went to school there and learned German, as well as how to get around London. But he moved back to Houston with his family in junior high.

Once he was back in the States, he became one of the top high school players in the nation. His international education also helped him get some great grades. When he graduated, he was named the co-valedictorian of his class—that meant he was one of the school's top students!

Andrew went on to Stanford University. At first, it looked like an odd pick. Their team was 1–11 the year before he started. But Stanford is one of the top universities in the world, and Andrew knew a degree from there would be important. Of course, the fact that the team had a new coach in former NFL quarterback Jim Harbaugh helped.

In three seasons as the starter at Stanford, Andrew took the team to three bowl games and finished second in the Heisman Trophy voting twice! And he got that degree he wanted, in architecture.

But another job was waiting for him after graduation: NFL quarterback. He was taken "number one" in the 2012 NFL draft by the Indianapolis Colts. All he had to do there was take over for Peyton Manning! That's a pretty tall order, but Andrew has been up to the task. He set an NFL rookie record with 4,374 passing yards, then set a team record in 2014 with 4,761 yards. Indy has won eleven games in each of his three seasons, and they've gone one game farther in the playoffs each year. At this pace, look for Indy in Super Bowl 50.

Football FACT

When a quarterback like Andrew leaves the pocket when being chased, it's called scrambling. But when he runs forward on purpose after dropping back, that is called a quarterback draw.

Andrew Luck

Height:	6' 4"
Weight:	240 ibs
College:	Stanford
Drafted:	2012

► STATS!

Attempts:	1,813
Completions:	1,062
Passing Touchdowns:	86
Passing Yards:	12,957

ANDREW LUCK

The 2014 Seahawks were struggling. The defending Super Bowl champs had started the season 4–3. Some people were saying they were not the same team. Fans were worried that there would be no repeat trip to the big game.

One of the biggest weapons in the Seattle offense was not firing on all cylinders. Marshawn Lynch had scored only three touchdowns in the team's first seven games. He had only one game with 100-plus yards. Was something wrong with the player who usually played in "Beast Mode"?

But in Week 8, things turned around. Lynch scored twice and the Seahawks won their fifth game. The following week, in a 38–17 thrashing of the Giants, Lynch scored a career-high four touchdowns and ran for 140 yards. The Beast was back! Seattle lost only one more game the rest of the season and earned that return trip to the Super Bowl. Though Lynch was the game's leading rusher with 102 yards and a touchdown, Seattle lost, 28–24, to New England. Many thought the game should have ended with Lynch getting one more carry to try to score. But Seattle chose a pass play and it was intercepted at the goal line.

For Lynch, the road to the Super Bowl started in California's San Francisco Bay Area. He was a high school star in Oakland. Then he played college football at nearby Berkeley, where he was an All-America player and the Pac-12 Offensive Player of the Year. His next stop on the road to the top was Buffalo, where he played for the Bills for three seasons.

In Seattle's run-heavy offense, Lynch was the workhorse and the star. He topped 1,200 yards in each of his four seasons in the Pacific Northwest. In 2013 and 2014, he led the NFL in rushing touchdowns.

Why Beast Mode? Lynch is nearly silent off the field with reporters. But when he's on the field, he has a different gear. When it's time to gain the tough yards, he seems to turn up his dials and power through any defense. Clearly one of the NFL's top runners, Lynch has been the key to Seattle's run to the top.

Football FACT

You can tell what formation Seattle uses by where Lynch lines up. Directly behind Russell Wilson? That's the I formation. Behind and to the left? That's the Pro Set. Directly behind, but with four wideouts? Call that the Spread.

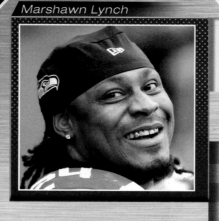

Marshawn Lynch

Height:	5' 11"
Weight:	215 lbs
College:	University of California, Berkeley
Drafted:	2007

▶ STATS!

Rushing Yards:	8,695
Receiving Yards:	1,899
Rushing Touchdowns:	71
Receiving Touchdowns:	9

MARSHAWN LYNCH

17

PEYTON MANNING

Even the greatest players face problems. For Peyton Manning, that came in 2011, when he hurt his neck. It looked for a while as if his great NFL career might have to end. He had surgery to fix the injury, but it took many months to recover. He could have just said that he'd had enough. He was already clearly headed to the Hall of Fame. He had his Super Bowl ring. Why keep playing?

But what he did next is what separates Manning from even the greatest players. He was away from the game for more than a year, but he battled back. And at age thirty-seven, in his fourteenth season, he set a single-season record with 55 touchdown passes.

But doing great things is nothing new for Manning. He grew up in New Orleans, where his father, Archie, had been a star quarterback for the hometown Saints. Peyton Manning was a high school superstar and chose Tennessee for his college ball. All he did there was make the Volunteers a top-five team and finish second in the Heisman Trophy voting.

The Colts made him the number-one overall pick in 1998 and he turned that team around.

While he was a Colt, he led the NFL in passer rating and touchdown passes three times, and passing yards twice. He carried them to the team's first Super Bowl victory in thirty-six years when they won Super Bowl XLI over the Bears in the 2005 season.

A strong arm, great leadership, and ability to pick just the right play: Manning did it all. But then the neck injury kept him out for all of 2011. The Colts had to let him go and move on. It was hard, but they felt they had to do it.

The Denver Broncos believed Manning had more in him. Boy, were they right! Manning has led Denver to three straight AFC West titles and at least a dozen wins. And there was that magical 2013 season when he crushed the old single-season touchdown mark by 5. And then he topped even himself in 2014. With an eight-yard pass to Demaryius Thomas, Manning became the NFL's all-time career leader in touchdown tosses. He ended the 2014 season with an amazing 530.

With all that Manning has done so far, who knows what else he can do?

Football FACT

The name "quarterback" comes from the old way teams lined up. Three players were behind the line of scrimmage. The fullback was farthest back, then the halfback a little closer, and finally, the quarterback. In those days, the quarterback almost never got the ball: he was a blocker!

Peyton Manning

Height:	6' 5"
Weight:	230 lbs.
College:	Tennessee
Drafted:	1998

▶ STATS!

Attempts:	9,049
Completions:	5,927
Passing Touchdowns:	530
Passing Yards:	69,691

PEYTON MANNING

19

JORDY NELSON

Hard work is nothing new for Jordy Nelson. In fact, playing football might just be a tad easier than the kind of work he did while growing up on a wheat farm in Kansas. Nelson fixed fences, drove a tractor, and herded cattle. All that hard work then gave him a desire to succeed that has made him one of the NFL's top receivers.

In high school, Nelson played quarterback, not receiver. No big colleges wanted him as their running quarterback. He went to school at Kansas State and walked on to the team. Coaches were amazed at his speed and skills. By his senior year, he was a star, with 122 catches and 11 touchdowns. He was chosen by the Packers in the second round in 2008.

But in the NFL, being fast is not enough. Nelson has worked hard to improve his routes and to learn more about how to get away from defensive backs. The strength built hauling hay is now used to push away from defenders or battle in the air for high balls.

The hard work on the football field has paid off. Nelson has increased his receiving yards in each of his full NFL seasons (he missed part of 2012 with an injury). He caught a career-high 1,519 yards in 2014 and earned his first Pro Bowl selection.

Nelson's nose for the end zone has become legendary. He has 43 touchdown catches in the past four seasons, second most among receivers in the NFL.

Nelson's breakout game came just at the right time. In Super Bowl XLV, he was originally going to be just a backup for Aaron Rodgers and the Packers. But Nelson slid into open spaces and caught nine passes for 140 big yards. The Kansas farm boy had become a Super Bowl champion. The following season, he became a full-time starter and had a career-high 15 touchdowns.

He almost got another chance at a ring in 2014. His Pro Bowl stats helped Green Bay make it to the NFC Championship Game. They came oh-so-close to winning, but fell to Seattle in overtime.

Between seasons, until the Packers need him in the end zone again, you can find Nelson back home, working in the field.

Football FACT

Most wide receivers in the NFL, including Nelson, have a little help. They wear special gloves that have a slightly sticky surface. The tight-fitting gloves still let the receivers "feel" the ball, but the stickiness helps those tough catches stay home.

Jordy Nelson

Height:	6' 3"
Weight:	217 lbs.
College:	Kansas State
Drafted:	2008

▶ STATS!

Receptions:	400
Touchdown Catches:	49
Receiving Yards:	6,109

JORDY NELSON

21

BEN ROETHLISBERGER

Talk about great beginnings: In the third game of 2004, Ben Roethlisberger took over as the Steelers' starting quarterback. He proceeded to lead the team to fourteen straight wins—an NFL first! Then he guided them to an overtime playoff win (before they lost the next week to the Patriots). With that beginning, Steelers fans expected big things from Big Ben. He has nearly always delivered, winning two Super Bowl championships in his first five seasons and helping the team reach the playoffs in five other seasons.

Roethlisberger joined the Steelers in 2004 after a record-setting career at Miami of Ohio. He was a rare combination of size and mobility. He weighs as much or more than the linemen trying to tackle him, and his height lets him see far downfield. At first, the Steelers relied on a running game, but over time, Roethlisberger's arm has become their main weapon. In his first five seasons, he never topped 4,000 yards. In his most recent six, he has gone over that mark four times. In fact, Roethlisberger had his career high in 2014 with 4,952, which also was the first time he led the league in that stat.

Though that was his best personal season, his two best team seasons were 2005 and 2008. As a second-year pro in 2005, Roethlisberger led the Steelers to Super Bow XL, where they beat Seattle. Three years later, they were in Super Bowl XLIII. In that win over Arizona, Roethlisberger had a key touchdown pass.

After such a great 2014, Roethlisberger looks like he has a lot more in the tank. He and Steelers fans are all hoping that his future seasons are as great as his first one.

Football FACT

Ben's pretty tall, but he's not the tallest passer ever. Dan McGwire played briefly with the Seahawks and Dolphins. He stood six feet, eight inches! Denver's Brock Osweiler, at six feet, seven inches, was the tallest in the NFL in 2014.

Ben Roethlisberger

Height:	6' 5"
Weight:	240 lbs.
College:	Miami of Ohio
Drafted:	2004

▶ STATS!

Attempts:	4,954
Completions:	3,157
Passing Touchdowns:	251
Passing Yards:	39,057

BEN ROETHLISBERGER

23

TERRELL SUGGS

● BALTIMORE RAVENS

LINEBACKER

Terrell Suggs plays linebacker, but in most games, he spends his time putting linemen—and quarterbacks—on their backs. Since bursting onto the NFL scene with a fantastic rookie season, he has been one of the top pass-rushers on one of the NFL's most accomplished defensive teams.

Suggs was born in Minnesota, but grew up in Arizona. There he became one of the nation's top defensive high school players. He was named All-America by *USA Today*. He moved on to Arizona State, where he continued to shine. He set a record with 24 sacks in 2002, the most ever in a single season by an NCAA player.

The Baltimore Ravens already had one of the best defenses in the NFL, led by the great Ray Lewis. Suggs, however, wasted no time making his mark on the NFL. In 2003, he had 12 sacks and was named the NFL Defensive Rookie of the Year. He was named to the first of what would become six Pro Bowls.

Over the next few seasons, Suggs, Lewis, and their teammates formed an imposing defensive wall. The Ravens were often among the league leaders in fewest points and fewest yards allowed. In 2011, Suggs had his best overall season. He led the team again with 14 sacks, while also intercepting a pair of passes and forcing an amazing 7 fumbles.

But the peak of Suggs's career to date certainly came in 2012. Already a veteran and a record-setter, he didn't have that championship ring. But Baltimore put it all together that year. Its defense was already strong, but it finally had a high-scoring offense, too. Though Suggs had to miss the first six games with an injury, he was back for the end of the year and for the playoffs. When the Ravens hoisted the Vince Lombardi Trophy after defeating the 49ers, Suggs was rightfully in the middle of the celebration.

Blessed with speed and quickness, Suggs has added experience to his list of qualities. Ever since Lewis left the team, he has become the leader of a still-solid defense.

Football FACT

Terrell has been selected to six Pro Bowls, which is pretty impressive. The record for most Pro Bowls by a linebacker is twelve, shared by fellow Raven Ray Lewis and Chargers great Junior Seau.

TERRELL SUGGS

Height:	6' 3"
Weight:	260 lbs.
College:	Arizona State
Drafted:	2003

▶ **STATS!**

Tackles:	511
Sacks:	106.5
Interceptions:	7

TERRELL SUGGS

25

JULIUS THOMAS

You can't play football by yourself. You need teammates to block or tackle or get you the ball. Julius Thomas knows that better than anyone. For his first two seasons in Denver, he was almost invisible. He made a grand total of one catch and didn't score. But then along came a guy named Peyton Manning.

Thomas grew up in central California and he was a star athlete . . . in another sport. At 6' 5", he was one of the top basketball players in the state. Then he headed to Portland State expecting to play only basketball, too. But the football team there needed some help. And the coaches saw this big, athletic guy and thought, "Hey, he could be a tight end." It was not impossible. Pro Bowl stars Antonio Gates and Tony Gonzalez switched from hoops to football.

So after setting a school record by playing in 121 basketball games, Thomas switched gears—and gear—and joined the football team. Turned out to be a good move. He was named all-conference after gaining 453 receiving yards. The Broncos saw the possibilities in this raw player and chose him in the fourth round in 2011.

However, he had so much to learn—plus, he suffered an ankle injury in 2012—and he got very little playing time.

But in 2012, the great Peyton Manning had joined the Broncos and everything changed. Manning loved having a big tight end to throw to. When he recovered from the ankle injury, the lessons Thomas had learned in two years of practice paid off. Seemingly out of nowhere, he snagged 12 touchdown passes and made the Pro Bowl in 2013. In 2014, with defenses now ready to stop this surprise star, he caught another dozen scoring passes.

In March of 2015, Thomas signed with the Jaguars, where his athletic abilities will certainly continue to shine!

Football FACT

Have you heard of the "fade"? Thomas and quarterback Peyton Manning have used this play often and well. It's used near the goal line. At the snap, Thomas runs toward the corner of the end zone. Manning lofts the ball in a high arc. Ideally, Thomas uses his height to outjump the cornerback and make the catch.

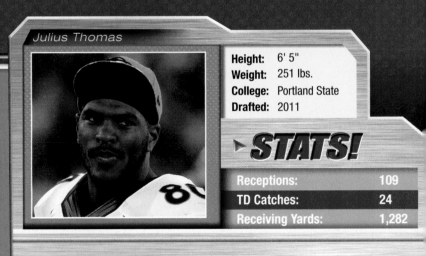

Julius Thomas

Height:	6' 5"
Weight:	251 lbs.
College:	Portland State
Drafted:	2011

▶ STATS!

Receptions:	109
TD Catches:	24
Receiving Yards:	1,282

JULIUS THOMAS

J. J. WATT

It's almost not fair. First, J. J. Watt becomes the dominant defensive player in the NFL. He wins two Defensive Player of the Year awards (2012, 2014), is the first player ever with two seasons with 20 or more sacks, and becomes a pass-swatting machine. In fact, his 33 deflections since 2011 are more than any other player. So what's not fair? Now he's also beating teams by scoring touchdowns!

For a player who is now an annual Pro Bowl selection, Watt had a slow start in football. He was actually a star hockey player as a kid growing up in Wisconsin. It wasn't until he grew to 6' 2" in high school that football became part of his year, and even then he was mostly a tight end. That's the position he played at Central Michigan University for a year, but he wasn't happy. He switched to the University of Wisconsin. Watt was a second-team All-America pick by his junior year. Next stop: the NFL.

Watt made a big impact on the Texans. He was a starter right away. The team needed him. They had been nearly at the bottom of the NFL defensive rankings. One year with Watt and they were near the top. The next year, 2012, he led the NFL with 20.5 sacks, tied for the fourth-highest total ever. He got that big award and made his first Pro Bowl. He was among the NFL's best again in 2013.

But in 2014, Watt added a scoring threat to his many football talents. Watt scored one of his touchdowns the usual way for a defender. He tipped a pass and then returned the interception for a score. A few games later, he picked up a fumble and ran 80 yards for another touchdown. But what made his season really unusual was that he caught three touchdown passes! At 6' 5", he's bigger than most tight ends and certainly bigger than every defensive back. So Houston figured, why not give him a shot? They lined him up as a tight end in goal-line situations and lofted the ball his way. Good luck wrestling Watt for a football. He also has 12 forced fumbles and 11 fumble recoveries in his career.

The five scores in 2014 were the most by a defensive player since 1944. And to make his season complete, he recorded his first safety.

Sacking machine, scoring machine—this mighty Texan can do it all.

Football FACT

Defensive stars like Watt have been tackling quarterbacks since the NFL began. But the sack has only been an official stat since 1982. How do you get 0.5, or half, of a sack? If two or more players knock down the quarterback at the same time, the stat master can award each player half a sack.

J. J. Watt

Height:	6' 5"
Weight:	290 lbs.
College:	Wisconsin
Drafted:	2011

▶ STATS!

Tackles:	241
Sacks:	57.0
Forced Fumbles:	12

J. J. WATT

ROOKIE RECEIVERS!

In 2014, NFL quarterbacks aimed passes at some of the best rookie receivers in a long time. Many first-year pass-catchers had big impacts on their team. One of them even turned in what most people called the "play of the year"!

ODELL BECKHAM JR
NEW YORK GIANTS

Leaping high above a Dallas defender on Thanksgiving Day, Beckham snagged a pass with one hand while reaching behind his head! The acrobatic catch was good for a touchdown and put Beckham on the big-play map. But it was just one part of a great rookie season for the former LSU player. After not even playing for the team's first four, he put together the best twelve-game run of stats for any rookie in NFL history—91 catches for 1,305 yards and 12 touchdowns.

KELVIN BENJAMIN
CAROLINA PANTHERS

Benjamin ended his college career by catching the pass that won Florida State the national championship. He started his pro career by finally giving Cam Newton a big target. Benjamin caught 73 passes in the season, including 9 for touchdowns. His 6' 5" height gave him a big advantage in the end zone, leaping above defenders.

MIKE EVANS
TAMPA BAY BUCCANEERS

In college, Evans was part of a high-scoring Texas A&M team that loved to pass. Moving to the NFL, he was not sure he'd get as many chances in the Buccaneers' run-oriented system. But with a talent like Evans, the Bucs made changes. Featured in their offense, he had 68 catches, including 12 for touchdowns, and showed speed and skill that will make him a star for a long time.

SAMMY WATKINS
BUFFALO BILLS

The Bills gave up a lot to get Watkins, including their first-round pick in 2015, but they got a lot in return. He hauled in 65 catches for nearly 1,000 yards and scored 6 times. Only the Bills' shaky quarterback situation kept him from doing even better. Watkins is a great deep threat who will surely see the end zone over and over again.

2014 NFL STANDINGS

AFC EAST

PATRIOTS	12-4
BILLS	9-7
DOLPHINS	8-8
JETS	4-12

AFC NORTH

STEELERS	11-5
BENGALS	10-5-1
RAVENS	10-6
BROWNS	7-9

AFC SOUTH

COLTS	11-5
TEXANS	9-7
JAGUARS	3-13
TITANS	2-14

AFC WEST

BRONCOS	12-4
CHIEFS	9-7
CHARGERS	9-7
RAIDERS	3-13

NFC EAST

COWBOYS	12-4
EAGLES	10-6
GIANTS	6-10
REDSKINS	4-12

NFC NORTH

PACKERS	12-4
LIONS	11-5
VIKINGS	7-9
BEARS	5-11

NFC SOUTH

PANTHERS	7-8-1
SAINTS	7-9
FALCONS	6-10
BUCCANEERS	2-14

NFC WEST

SEAHAWKS	12-4
CARDINALS	11-5
49ERS	8-8
RAMS	6-10

● SUPER BOWL XLIX
NEW ENGLAND PATRIOTS 28, SEATTLE SEAHAWKS 24